CELTIC DESIGN

Aidan Meehan studied Celtic art in Ireland and Scotland and
has spent the last two decades playing a leading role in the
renaissance of this authentic tradition. He has given workshops,
demonstrations and lectures in Europe and the USA, and more
recently throughout the Pacific North West from his home
base in Vancouver, B.C., Canada

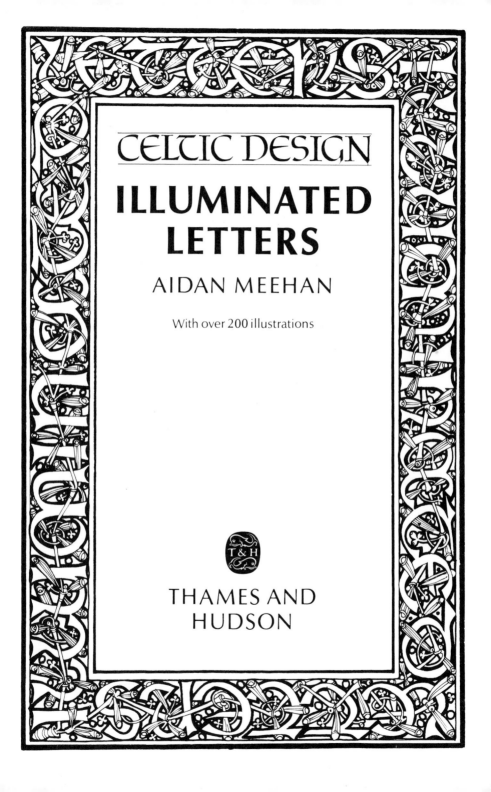

CELTIC DESIGN

ILLUMINATED LETTERS

AIDAN MEEHAN

With over 200 illustrations

THAMES AND
HUDSON

This Book is Dedicated to Danu

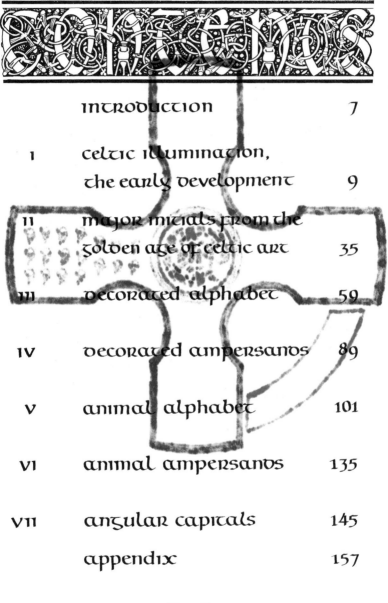

Contents

[5]

[6]

※

OOKS ABOUT CELTIC
illumination usually pre-
sent us with colour repro-
ductions that focus on the
most elaborate examples as tightly pack-
ed with details as a Persian carpet. This
book is a collection of simpler ornamental letters picked out and rendered as
line drawings, ready to be coloured.
As such it is a resource for Celtic artists, calligraphers and crafts people,
and indeed anybody that shares an in-
terest in the inventiveness of the Celtic

scribes. In their own day, there must have been reference manuals, similar to studio text books, passed down from one generation to the next. I hope this series will serve in the same way for a new generation.

⁘

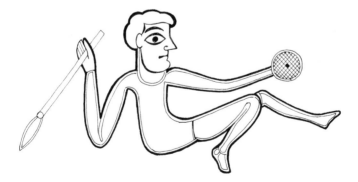

CELTIC ILLUMINATION, THE EARLY DEVELOPMENT

 VERY EARLY PSALM BOOK, the Cathach of St Columba, c. 600, is decorated with letters in Irish script treated with spirals of a pure Celtic style. Some have small animal heads, fish perhaps, and crosses of a type found in sixth-century Ireland. It is the earliest surviving evidence of the first developments of Celtic illumination. The letters are built up with broad and narrow penstrokes in a dark brown ink, with red dots outlining the shape and yellow voids inside the letters.

Fig.1 Letter M from the Cathach.

Even in black and white as in this M, the dots add a half-tone which heightens the white voids between the penstrokes of the curves, and between the spirals and the styl-ized birdhead terminals. The split curves form moons; the terminals are an ancient Celtic art motif, called divergent trum-pet pattern.

Fig.2 Letter Q, the Cathach.

In this built-up black letter, the split of the curves has been reduced to a sliver of a moon, toned down even further by hatching. From the spiral foot leaps a long-jawed, fish-like creature, a dolphin perhaps, bearing a cross. Two curves on its neck might be read as gills. Its laughing mouth is a black sub-triangle relieved by a white lens, another detail of Celtic spiral treatment.

Fig. 3 Natural uncials, Luxeuil c. 600.

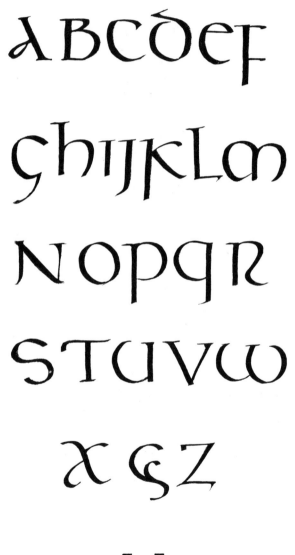

Fig.4 Irish half-uncials. Bobbio c.600.

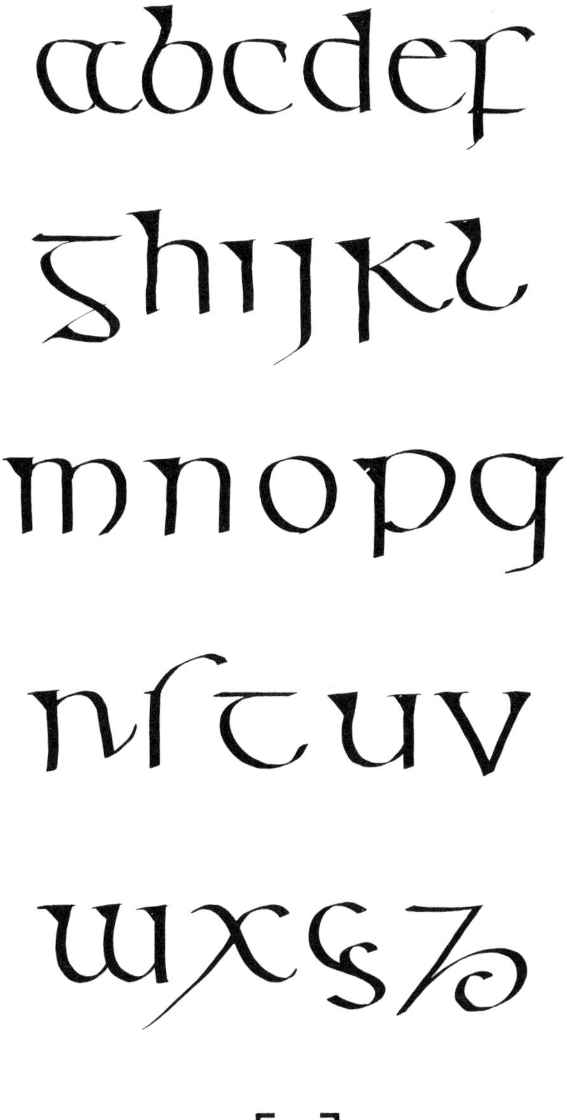

abcdef

ghijkl

mnopq

nʃtuv

wxyz⁊

FIG. 5 Monogram DS , the Cathach.

I inmomine

·X· & : in uirtute

DS exaudionationem

THIS UNCIAL D has a fish tail with a
pelta, diverging to a trumpet opposite a plain divergence that counters curve
with corner, ending in a discreet spiral. Inside, a red dot-and-slash filler, a main-
stay of Celtic ornament for centuries.

R ED dotting is the first stage of illumi-
nating Celtic letters. Rubrication, as
this is called, adds a dimension of colour to
that of contrast. The effect is that of a tint:
by breaking up the red with white inter-
spaces, the eye mixes the solid colour with
the gaps to perceive pink. Dotting makes
the letter appear to float up off the page and
glow rosily. The letters D and S of *fig.*5
may be dotted using *fig.*1 as a guide.
Trace around the letters with a light
pencil line first, then dot along the line,
and erase it. Use a fine-tip red marker.
A NOTHER FEATURE of Celtic illumination is called the *diminuendo,*
where the large capital is led into harmony
with the text by an intermediate letter or

FIG.6 NOLI , the Cathach.

Nemulani
Neq: zelauerir
quoniamtam quam fenum
& quem ab modum holena herb

letters, smaller than the initial, but larger
than the text. The Cathach is a very early
example of this, *fig.6*. The space between the
uprights of the N features a long-stemmed
cross combining both the Greek and the Ro-
man form. Below the cross the bar of the
letter undulates, and suggests the form of a
fish. But as well as the obvious symbols,
there is a geometric, numerical symbol in

the way the diminuendo forms a 3: 4 triangle. These two numbers are significant as
relating to the Trinity and the cross, but also
as they sum up to seven, the symbolic theme
of the Book of Revelation of St John, who
saw seven golden candlesticks, and in their
midst a lamb with seven horns and seven
eyes, who said

> I am the Alpha and the Omega,
> the beginning and the end,
> the first and the last.

ALPHA AND OMEGA turn up in another early Gospelbook, the
Codex *Usserianus*, named after the seven-
teenth century Dubliner, Bishop Ussher.
It provides a clue to the type of full-page
design that may once have served as a
frontispiece for Celtic manuscripts at the
end of the sixth century. The Ussher Codex contains such a page in the form of
the monogram X-P, or *Chi-Rho*, outlined
in dots, *fig*. 7. The Greek letter X is rotated into a cross with a shaft twice as
long as the transverse, and divided by it
so that it suggests the three-in-one with
equal units above and below the middle
bar. The page has been ruled with lines
scored beforehand as for a page of text;
the centre square is 12 ruled spaces deep.

Fig. 7 Cross-monogram page, Usher Codex, c. 600.

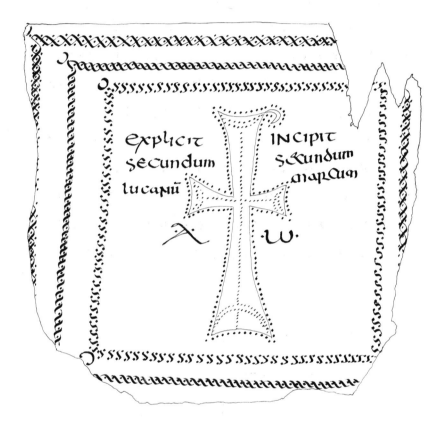

explicit
secundum
lucanu

INCIPIT
secundum
marcum

Fig.8 Pattern of the Usshen monogram.

In the upper left is the Latin word Explicit, which means, here ends (Luke). This is balanced diagonally opposite, at bottom right, by the Greek letter W, Omega, which means the end (or last letter of the alphabet).

In the upper right, Incipit – here begins (Mark), is mirrored lower left by Alpha, the beginning (of the alphabet), recalling the words of the Book of Revelation, I am the Alpha and the Omega, the beginning and the end.

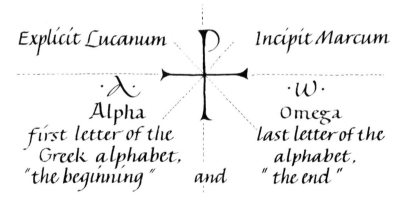

Explicit Lucanum · · Incipit Marcum

·λ·
Alpha
first letter of the
Greek alphabet,
"the beginning"   and

·W·
Omega
last letter of the
alphabet,
" the end "

THE DIVISION OF THE CROSS SHAFT by the arm in the ratio 1:2 refers to the creation of the two, heaven and earth, by the one, God. The horizontal arm moves between the two parts as in Genesis 1:2, where "the Spirit of God moved upon the waters". Then follow the seven days of Creation, each a pair of opposites: Day and Night; waters above and below the firma — ment; Earth and Seas; Sun and moon; birds and animals; Adam and Eve. God rested on the seventh day, symbol- ized as the still centre of a circle divid- ed by its radius. Thus not only the number seven but also the hexagonal marigold motif of *fig.* 10 are symbols of the birth of the cosmos.

THE USSHER MONOGRAM PAGE is an intentional play of number symbols; for example, the 1:2 proportion of the cross width to height, as we have seen. This is also the ratio of the two strokes of letter *chi*, or *X*, where the thin is twice as long as the thick one. In the monogram the diagonal cross, *chi*, is rotated to become the upright cross. However, the pattern of the diagonals is emphasized in the pattern of the inscription *fig.8*. But the upright cross introduces its own symbolism, foursquare, and quarter. The pattern of the text is divided left and right, Luke and Mark; and also above and below, Latin overhead, Greek beneath.

APART FROM THIS BILINGUAL PLAY there is the reference to the Revelation of St John, Alpha and Omega, which is associated with the number seven that links the first book of the Old Testament with the last book of the New Testament. The cross in the centre of the square is naturally fourfold, but its proportions of 2:1 make it tripartite. The pattern of the text supports this three- and fourfoldness, for there are four lines of writing divided into three in the upper quadrant and one in the lower, a trinity symbol, 3:1. As well, the text is divided symmetrically into two pillars flanking the vertical axis of the cross shaft, and with it make three columns altogether.

FIS.9   Dot-and-stroke pattern, Ussher.

Start with a single row of dots, then add the
stroke. Think of the spot as the centre of a circle,
and the stroke follows the curve over the one
and under the next.

Start with two rows of dots. This pattern de-
pends on a sharp contrast between thick and
thin , a basic broad nib exercise.

Start with two rows, then add the third as
the centre of each square cell. Or think of it as
a five-spot if you prefer. Do one zig-zag,
then put in the second.

chi   First zig-zag   Second zig-zag

THREE AND FOUR RECUR IN THE BORDER, *fig.* 9, where we see the middle border is a pattern based on a single row of dots and horizontal s-scroll pen strokes; the inside border based on two dots and a vertical s-scroll ; the outer border based on three rows, a synthesis of saltire and diamond forming a two-strand helix . So we have a trinity of square borders, the outermost a repeat of the saltire and dots, ✕ as used in *fig.* 5, line 2, a Cathach contraction for Christ. The corners of the squares are decorated with horns, twelve in all; there are twelve sides in all, as in the edges of a cube; the ground plan of the centre area is twelve square. Twelve and seven, 3x4 and 3+4, numbers of the New Jerusalem and Genesis are the themes used here.

FIG.10 Carpet page, Chronicle of Orosius,
Showing Geometry.

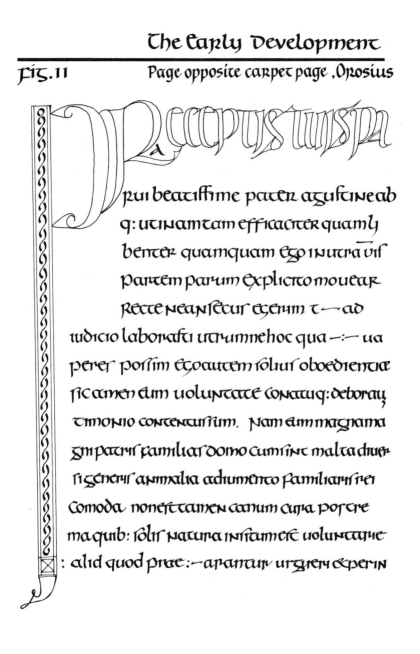

Pru beatiffime pater aguftineab
q: utinam tam efficaciter quamly
benter quamquam ego inutra uī
partem parum explicito mouear
Recte neanfecut egerim τ ̄ ad
iudicio laborafu utrumnehoc qua ∴ ua
perer poffim egoautem foluif oboedientic
fic amen cum uoluntate Conatuq: deboray
timonio contentufum. Nam cum magnama
gm patrif familiaf domo cumfint malta diuer
figenerif animalia achumento familiarifrei
comoda noneft tamen catrum cura porcre
ma quib: folif natura inftamet uoluntatue
: alid quod prae ∶ apantur urgrem experin

THE NEXT MAJOR DEVELOPMENT was the full-page ornament facing a page-length initial followed by a banner headline extending to the right-hand margin. This combination became the trademark of seventh-century Celtic manuscripts, but we find a prototype in the copy of the Chronicle of Orosius, from the Columban foundation of Bobbio, written about 620 in an early script like that of the Ussher Codex. The full-page pattern is based on a 10 x 12 square grid, as shown in *fig. 10*. The 3 x 4 theme which we found in the Ussher Codex turns up here in the construction of the circles, as in *fig. 12*. The four corner circles each have 3 rings; the centre circle has 8 rings, with seven interstitial bands.

Fig. 12   Geometry of Chronicle of Orosius.

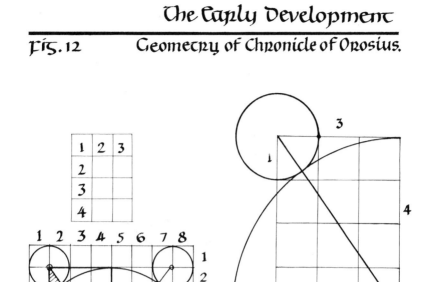

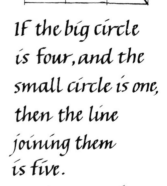

If the big circle
is four, and the
small circle is one,
then the line
joining them
is five.

However this diagonal is the longest side
of the right-angle triangle shown shaded,
which therefore has sides 3 x 4 x 5.

Fi5.13   Merovingian letter N,
          Commentary of St. Jerome.

Fig.14   Initial page from Durham Fragment II.

THE OPENING UP OF THE LETTERFORM
introduces fresh scope for ornament,
in the body of the letter itself. We now have
a new order of initial. In the Chronicle of
Orosius, a two-cord braid fills the descender. Although it is applied as an after-
thought, by the rubricator, the idea of
decorating the letter with a two-cord
braid quickly spread from scribe to scribe.
and soon made its appearance as an integ-
ral part of the pen-drawn letter, as we
can see from a fragment of a Gospel book
that apparently came to the cathedral
library of Durham from elsewhere,
fig.14, but cannot be much later than its
prototype from Bobbio of c.620, fig.13. In
this example from a Commentary of St.Jer-
ome, we find the short ascender has been

divided into four boxes, separated by three lines. In the Durham fragment, *fig 14*, the ascender is divided into four parts separated by two lines. Both have spiral serifs. Both have animal cross-bars, the pair from Durham have gills, clearly referring to fish. The fish in the Bobbio example leap out of a *chi*-cross centrepiece, based on the form of the letter, χ, the curves drawn out as spirals. The eels of Durham are centred on the cursive, minuscule letter, $\varkappa$, the multiplication sign. The style of the two letters is different, that of Bobbio is Merovingian, and the one from Durham is Celtic. But the similarities are so striking, they must have a common model.

Chapter 1

WHAT WE SEE IN THE DURHAM fragment from the first quarter of the seventh century is the beginning of the synthesis of ornamental forms from many different sources encountered, col‐lected and copied by the scribes on their travels abroad. Now a shift of empha‐sis took place, away from the monastery as a communal sanctuary of ascetics to‐wards a training ground for evangelism. Whereas before, the art of illumination had hidden itself from the eyes of the world, now it increasingly had to be attractive ; no longer the monopoly of the scribes, for artisans were begin‐ning to elaborate on the basic ele‐ments, the new art was about to spring into the light of day .

※

MAJOR INITIALS from the GOLDEN AGE of CELTIC ART

HE BOOK OF DURROW represents the first flowering of the tradition in the early seventh century when the ornament was mainly spiral and knotwork, figs 15,16. Here we see the letters outlined and filled with knot borders, while the serifs and voids are filled with Celtic spirals derived from ancient metalwork patterns: divergent trumpets and occasional horse-head terminals.

Fig.15   Letters F and Q, from the Book of Durrow.

THE amazing thing about the Book of Durrow is its scale, only 9½ x 6½ in (24 x 16.5 cm), not much larger than this book. The letters of fig. 15 are reproduced to about the same size, drawn with a fine nib and hairline brush in the original, though I have used technical pens here. The letters were drawn in a brownish black, like the patina in the sunken back – grounds of gold brooches, and coloured with a bright, cold lemon – yellow tempera, imitating gold inlaid with enamel, with warm plum–red and deep copper–green. To people unaccustomed to painting it must have looked magically realistic, akin to photo-realism today.

Fi5.16 Monogram IN, from the Book of Durrow.

FI5.17   Monogram INP, from Corpus Christi ms. 197.

FROM THE SEVENTH to the ninth century, artists and scribes travelled continually from one Celtic monastery to another, giving and exchanging books which were copied and recopied. The models were transmitted rapidly far and wide, new developments catching on alongside older forms, transitional designs appearing beside fixed conventions. Some decorators used designs learnt at school from older masters passing on motifs familiar to them from their own early days. Accordingly it is no surprise to see Durrow-style animals alongside birds of a generation later in the Corpus Christi College Library, ms. 197, *fig.* 17.

The knot at the bottom of the N in Corpus Christi turns up in the Book of Lindisfarne fifty years later, at the top of the same letter, as in *figs.*17,26. In Lindisfarne the knot is decked with dogheads whose ears connect in spirals, a trick inherited by MacRegol in his INP, *fig.* 18, a century later. An even greater span lies between the INP of Corpus Christi and that of MacRegol, so similar in design as to suggest a common model, *figs* 17, 18. MacRegol also preserves features of Durham II in the dog's tongue, *figs* 18,20; also, com – pare the knot of *figs* 19,20.

Fig.18

Monogram INP, from the Book of MacRegol.

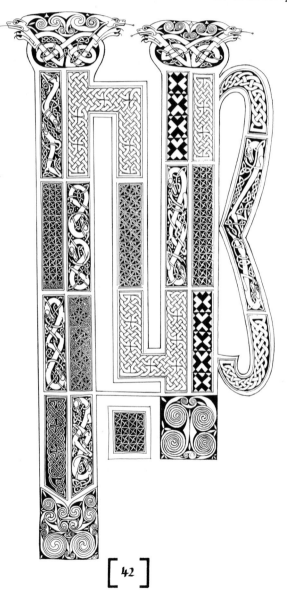

Another example of the diffusion of motifs, over time as well as distance, is the instance of the white curl at the nape of the neck of the dog and the bird heads of Durham II. This turns up in the Book of Kells, fig.47, in the late eighth century. A similar pattern of conservation and exchange of decorations occurring between many schools is found on the Continent, among those established by Irish monks of the sixth century. But with the Anglo-Irish foundation of Echternach, Celtic manuscripts were circulated throughout the seventh century such as we find at Cologne Cathedral and Trèves, St Gall and St Willibrord, figs 21-24.

Fig. 19   Monogram LIB, the Book of Mac Regol.

FIG.20   Letters A, M, from Durham Fragment II.

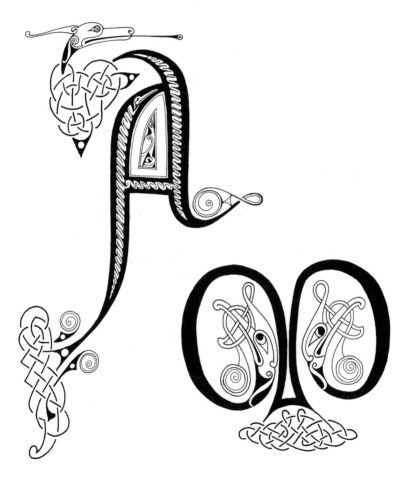

FIG. 21   letters D, D, from Cologne Cathedral ms. 213.

The manuscript from Cologne, fig. 21 has a fish tailed D like that of the Cathach, fig. 5, converted to black line knots as in Durham, fig. 20, and filled with spirals like that of fig. 27.

Fig.22   Letter N, from the Book of Trèves.

The Trèves N has no animals but for
this exception, with birdhead quad-
rupeds. The style is that of the time
of Durrow, but was written a century later at a monastery near Echternach.

F15.23   Letter Q . from the Book of St Gall.

FIG. 24 Letter Q from the Book of St Willibrord.

THE ANIMAL STYLE of the Book of Trèves is not unique. The Cologne manuscript also has a hybrid form, the long-beaked birdhead attached to quadruped hind legs, *fig. 21*. This style persists well into the eighth century on the Continent, a parallel development reflecting an influence other than Irish or Northumbrian : Pictish, for instance. Or it may represent a survival stemming from an early, cherished model ; or the result of a strong conservative tradition. Lacking animal patterns, the Book of Willibrord also known as the Book of Echternach did little to alter the influence of the early transitional style on the Continent , *fig. 24*.

FIG.25   MA and D, the Book of Lindisfarne.

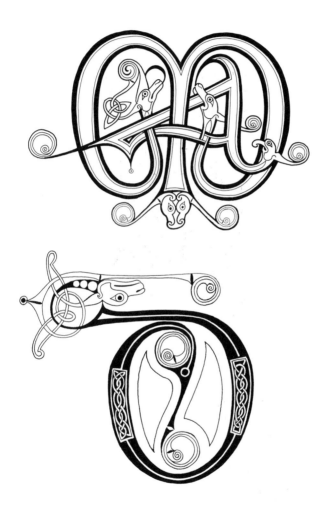

FIG. 26   Letter N, from Lindisfarne.

Here the spiral patterns are pure Celtic, very similar to those of Durrow. Also, compare the M of *fig*. 25 with that of *fig*. 20. The N of Lindisfarne, *fig*. 26, is filled with birds, a late seventh-century development.

Fig. 28 Letter M, from the Vatican

Barbarini ms. 570.

The tradition began to lapse in Eng -
land after the Book of Lindisfarne, as
seen by the Book of Cerne, fig. 29, and
the Book of Uigbald, abbot of Lindisfarne about 800, fig. 28.

FIG. 29   Letter A, from the Book of Cerne.

FIG. 30   Letter Q, from the Maihingen Gospels.

FIG.31   Letter X, from the Maihingen Gospels.

O N THE CONTINENT, however,
the Irish-Northumbrian fusion
epitomised by the Book of Lindisfarne
continued unabated in the eighth century as we have seen from the Book of
Trèves. In the Maihingen Gospels,
figs 30, 31 we see a fine example of
creative, original work which integrates
and ramifies the innovations of the
previous centuries, and so furthers
the tradition. But the best example
of this vitality and creativity, which
are so necessary to a living, growing
tradition is of course the Book of
Kells, to which we now turn in order
to understand the elements of Celtic
design as applied to decorated letters.

DECORATED ALPHABET

 HIS ALPHABET IS DRAWN from the Book of Kells (see reading list page 160). In the original each letter is finely dotted all around with red, closely following the outside of the letter about a millimetre from it, where the dots are of the same dimension, and the same distance apart. Enclosed areas are not dotted. The letters may be drawn with a wide-nibbed calligraphy pen, requiring manipulation, or drawn with a pencil and inked-in with a fine brush, such as a size zero sable. The ink to use is chinese black, softened with

the addition of a drop or so of vermilion and lemon yellow water colour. Paper should be a good quality, and extra-smooth, not very absorbent.

Opposite:

a

Tripartite division of enclosure provides a suggestion for void treatment of other letters, such as P or Q.

b

Central division a triangular pennant pan-elled with step pattern.

c

Pennant bracketed by birds; lionhead ter-minal biting lion cub.

d

Pennant emblazoned with a variant of the triquetra.

Fig. 32

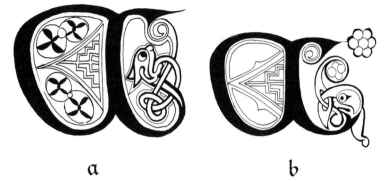

a

b

c

d

Fig. 33

The body spirals in a diamond forming a path of the open ground converging on a chevron arrowhead.

a   b

a

The C is continuous with the uncial A,
with lionhead and triquetra knot.

b

Two sub-semicircles filled with knotwork
frame an angular O containing an asterisk.

Fig. 35

Triangular flag-serif is decorated with
a spiral mask, with triskele eyes and a
marigold motif for a mouth. Inside, a
roundel of two lions.

Opposite: a
Here is a spiral spacefiller that could be adapted to letters b, c, p, q.

Fig.36

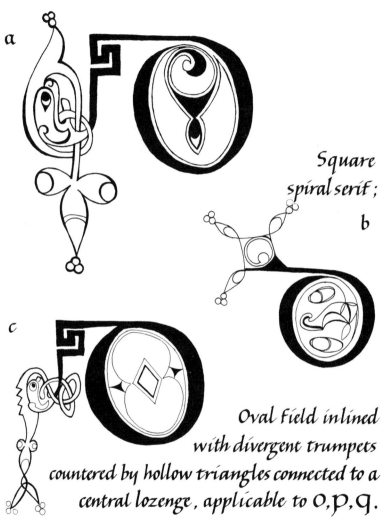

a

Square
spiral serif;

b

c

Oval field inlined
with divergent trumpets
countered by hollow triangles connected to a
central lozenge, applicable to O, p, q.

Fig. 37   Monograms EGO, ER, ERA, E.

a

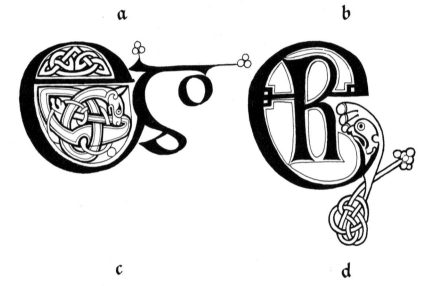

b

c

d

Previous page:

a

Triquetral dog pattern adapted from a roundel.

b

Lionhead terminal with carpet-beater knot.

c

The larger knot here is useful in a long triangular area like this.

d

Upper section inline relieved by divergent trumpets, useful treatment for filling a tight area, as in R. Lower, triquetra knot adapted to a semicircle.

OF ALL THE SURVIVING CELTIC
MANUSCRIPTS, our single most
valuable source of letter forms is the
Book of Kells, because it is so continuous-
ly decorated throughout. It is extraor-
dinary that between the two types of
letters collected here - the decorated black
letter and the animal alphabet which
were used interchangeably, we have al-
most the whole Latin alphabet; apart
from letters J and W, unknown to the
scribes, K and Y were rare. Not sur-
prisingly, no paragraphs in the Book of
Kells begin with X or Z. Otherwise, we
lack only letters F in this and G, M in
the animal alphabet.

This half-uncial G has a crossbar suitable for that of the letter T.

Overleaf:

a

An integration of serif and ponytail that would also work for uncial M.

b

Fine knot treatment for ascender serif, and a bearded head that might apply to a C.

Fig. 39

a

b

c

d

IH.

Fig.40

Split curve and back-
ward ascender are
both archaic features.
Compare fig. 39, a,b.

Previous page:

     c

Spiral lion
lacks forelegs. The supporting bird does not be-
long to the letter, but adds a decorative touch.

     d

Lion's-paw motif at the foot serif. The gap at
the base is bridged by the drunkard's-path
motif, as if the inline suffers a fear of open spaces.

Fig.41   Monogram ILL.

A chicken contemplates a swash knot ending
in a trefoil or a bunch of berries. The serifs have
the lion's-paw motif.
Two Ls, one with a drunkard's-path inline
and one without.

Fig.42 Three letters based on previous figure.

E ACH OF THE DECORATED LETTERS is unique, a variation on a theme, inviting further changes. Elements of one letter may be swapped for another. Serifs may be interchanged, mutated. You can take one ascender, one descender, one terminal, one ovoid and apply them to the letters of figs 3, 4, to make your own alphabet. Or make up your own letters.

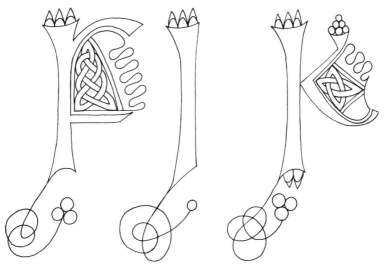

Fig. 43

This human head terminal could be adapted to a C or a K. The knot could also be used in an h or n.

Opposite: a

Knot work serifs with lion head descender. The serifs of the A are subtle, a synthesis of knot and spiral.

                              b

A fully decorated uncial N, with knotwork and single spirals, drunkard's-path, wheel-in-circle and step pattern brackets.

Fig. 44

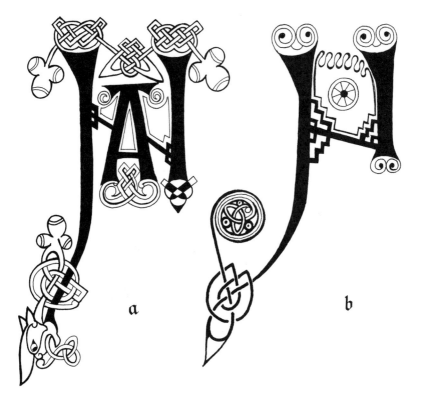

a   b

Monogram NA.

FIG.45

Perfectly symmetrical bird pattern roundel, adapted to internal ovoid.

Lion's tongue ends in a lentoid knot. Interior is filled with a pure Celtic spiral treatment.

Fig.46

The oval is filled with a beautiful spiral pattern, based on a regular circular design. The upper serif is a sitting duck. The lionhead serif has a curling lock of white-on-black typical of the Durham Fragment II, as in fig.20 above.

Fig. 47

Typical three-part division of the ovoid.
Spiral knot in serif with shamrocks.

Opposite:

a   Here triangle and trefoil combine.
b   This letter is pointed on the left-hand side.
c   Ovoid pattern of zigzag and arches.

Fig.48

a

b

c

Fig.49

a

b

c

d

e

FIG. 50   Monogram OR.

This left-hand corner is decorated with a knot
based on lozenge
and saltire,

called the
FORMA
FORMARUM,   or 'form of forms'.

Previous page :

Angular Q with fylfot-tile diaper and a
carpet-beater knot on the descender.
Also, four tile variations.

FIS. 51

Matching pair
with simple spirals.

a

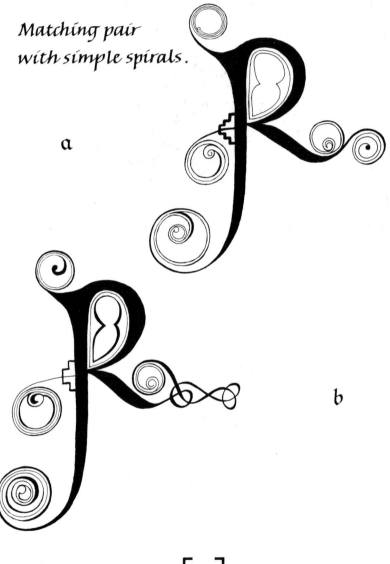

b

FIG.52

Hollow dart motif on head serif.

a

Lionhead foot
continues
up to spiral.

b

Fig. 53   Monogram SV   Monogram SCI

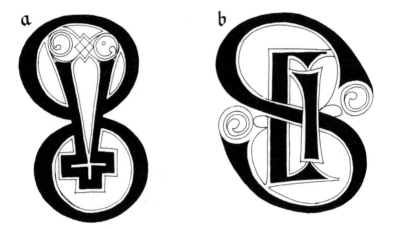

a

Pure abstract form, the waist of the S is hidden
by the superimposed V to make it appear like
two circles in a figure eight.

b

Monogram plainly outlined.

Fig. 54   Monogram TUN. Monogram TV.

a

This animal head has two long ears, eye presented frontally rather than in profile, and no line dividing the cheek from the jaw. This is how the hare is conventionally rendered.

b

Lion bites his own forelock.

Fig.55   Monogram VA. Monogram VI.

Integrated spirals
and knot
link the serifs.
The treatment
of the spirals
is unique.

a

The bird filler
would be good
in the upper part
of e.

b

a This lion head
sports a knot
which meta-
morphoses into
a spiral and a
tree-of-life
growing from
a horn-of-
plenty.

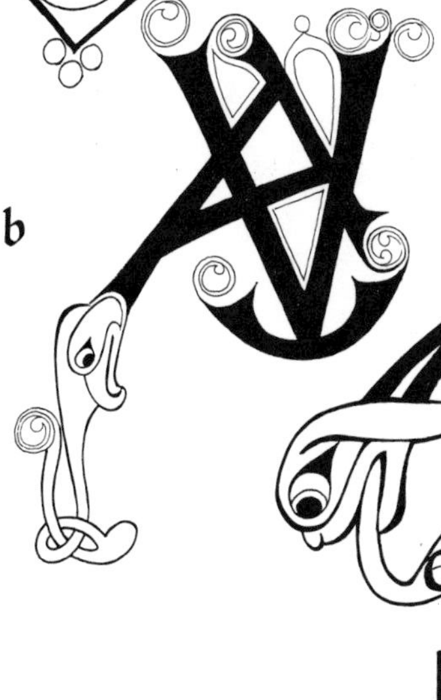

b

c

Another spiral-knot serif, this one very
subtly integrates with the inline of the
letter.

❈

DECORATED AMPERSANDS

 HE AMPERSAND is a com —
pound of two letters, Et, the
latin word Et, meaning and;
in the ampersand the cross-
bar of the E continues into the body of the
T, leaving the bar of the T hanging there.
The ampersand of today is a favourite of
letter artists for the wide variety of its
forms : & ; ℰ; ⅋ ;ℰ ; & ; eᴛ; ⅋. The Celtic
scribes obviously loved it too, and no-
where is it presented with so much of the
shape-shifter's art as in the Book of Kells,
from which these examples have been drawn.

Fig.58

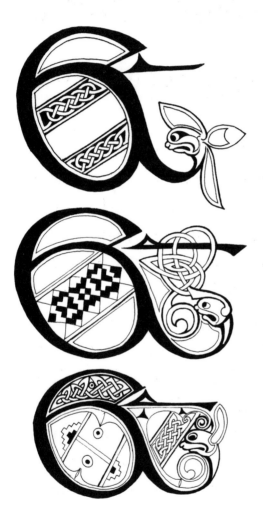

a

b

c

FIG.59

a

b

c

Fig. 60

a

b

c

Fig.61

a

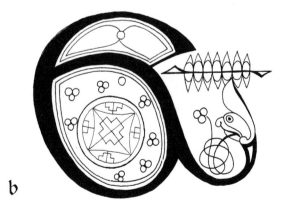

b

Fig.62

a

b

Fig.63

a

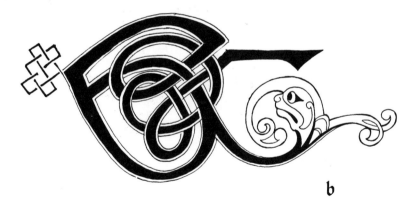

b

Fig. 64

a

b

Fig.65

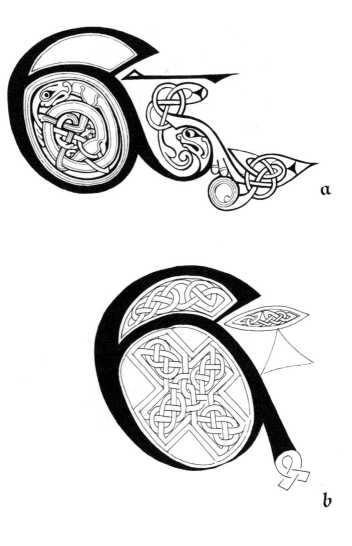

a

b

FIG. 66

a

b

AMPERSANDS PROVIDE A GREAT
BODY OF VARIATIONS on a single letter form, in this case the mono-gram ET. As we have seen above, page 73, a whole alphabet may be derived from just one or two decorated letters. This applies also to the ampersands on these pages. Each ampersand has a cross-bar with a serif and a terminal, except in a few cases where the bar is converted to a pure ornament, as *fig. 59 a*. The regular cross-bar treatments may be applied to the letter T or the half-uncial ȝ. Likewise, the terminal of the T part of the ampersand may be applied not only to T, but also to the other half-uncials that have corresponding terminals, such as

[*99*]

A.C.E.K.L.R.X.Z. Thus a lionhead terminal could be generalized throughout these letters, with variations from the wide range to choose in both this and in the previous chapter. Or we might instead choose a human-head terminal, fig. 62, or a rabbit-head terminal, fig. 63 a. In either case we should have a very different alphabet as a result. The E part of the ampersand contains a narrow void or half-lunette, which may be applied to E, or the loop of an R. The larger void may be applied to the half-uncials A, B, D, O, P, Q; the treatment of the open space between cross-bar and terminal may be applied to the letters C, K, T, X.

ANIMAL ALPHABET

 HIS ALPHABET also comes from the Book of kells, and may be used interchangeably with that of chapter III, as minor initials with a text of Irish half-uncials. These initials may be coloured with black ink backgrounds and a halo effect of red dots. Or you may want to paint the letter with tempera colours, as for example on the cover of this book. I drew these with technical pens, using a medium nib throughout, with fine nib inline and thick for outline.

Fig. 67

a   b

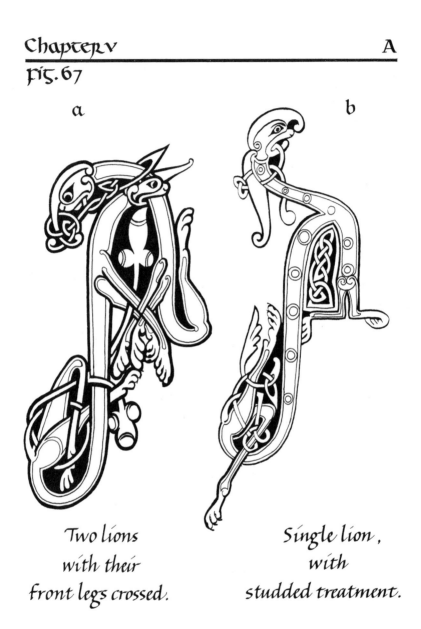

Two lions
with their
front legs crossed.

Single lion,
with
studded treatment.

fig.68

In the previous figure there are two approaches to animal lettering. In fig. 67 a, the letter is made up of two lions. In the accompanying letter, the letter is the main part, with a lion's head serif on the top, hind legs form a descender serif, and forelegs form the remaining serif. Here, the half-uncial is predominant, with the upper serif extended into hindquarters, the lower serif a lion's head. Overleaf, fig. 69 b is similarly constructed.

FIS. 69

Lappet from lion's crown

b

ends in a grape bunch!
Its tail tassel sprouts
three banded lobes.

a

This lion has hard—
ly any knots, in
contrast to this lion
and bird below.

c

fís. 70

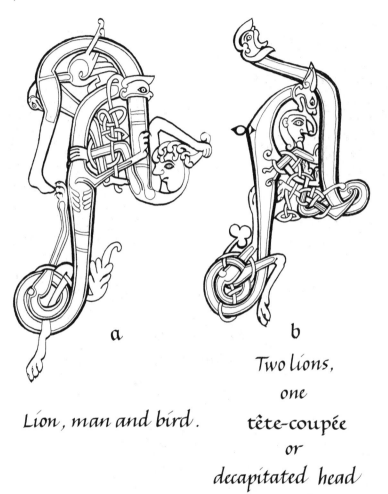

a

Lion, man and bird.

b

Two lions,
one
tête-coupée
or
decapitated head
motif.

Fig. 71

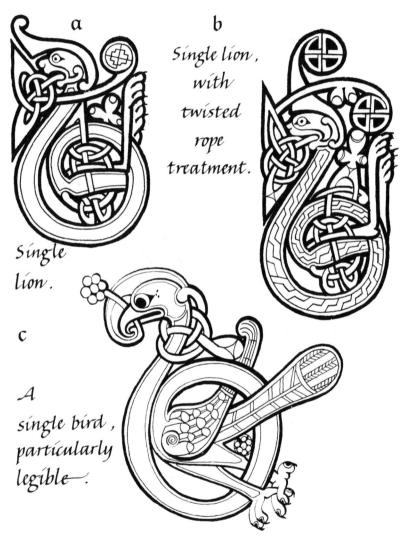

a

Single lion.

b

Single lion,
with
twisted
rope
treatment.

c

A
single bird,
particularly
legible.

Fig. 72

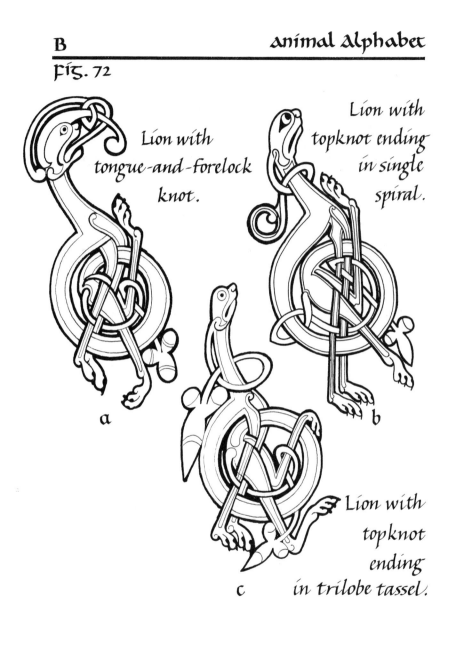

Lion with tongue-and-forelock knot.

a

Lion with topknot ending in single spiral.

b

Lion with topknot ending in trilobe tassel.

c

FIG. 73

In fig. 71 a,b we have seen two letters with lion heads corresponding to ascender serifs, and hind legs as terminals. These animals are incomplete, lacking forelegs! In fig. 72, we have the complete animal, as may be seen by turning the figure sideways. See how they run!

This lion's tail ends in a grape cluster.

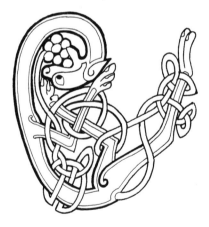

Fig. 74

You may have noticed that in the previous two chapters there were no birds, apart from one example in fig. 56 b. Likewise, in the animal alphabet, the bird assumes a secondary role, except for this one and its match, fig. 71 c. The bird is not as versatile as the quadruped, perhaps, but works well in a single serif letter here. It also might be applied to I, J, L, P, Q, U, V.

Fig. 75

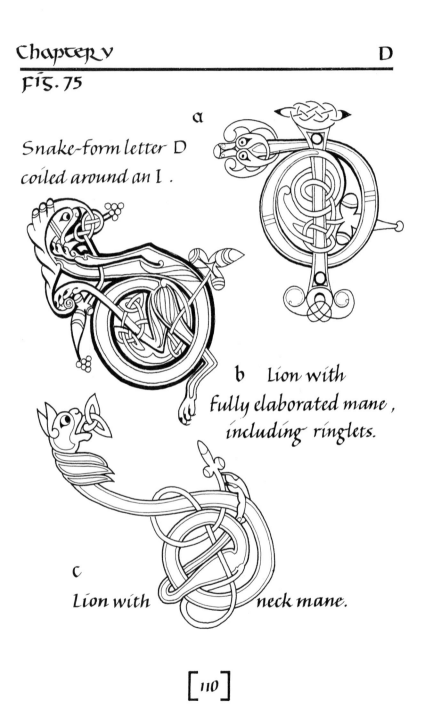

a

Snake-form letter D coiled around an I .

b Lion with fully elaborated mane, including ringlets.

c

Lion with   neck mane.

Fig. 76

a

A tabby cat, or lioness.

b

Snake.

c

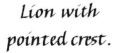

Lion with
pointed crest.

d

A griffin.

Fig. 77

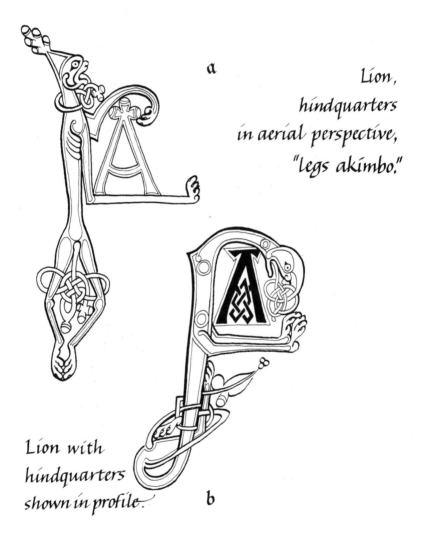

a

Lion,
hindquarters
in aerial perspective,
"legs akimbo."

Lion with
hindquarters
shown in profile.

b

Fig. 78

a

Lion with paw
extended
in the air.

b

Lion with striped
back and thighs.

Lion rampant , a basic ascender.

Fig. 80

Lion with crescentic ears, shoulder mane pattern
and crescent ribs.

Fig. 81

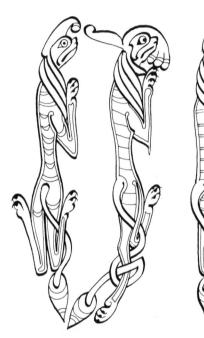

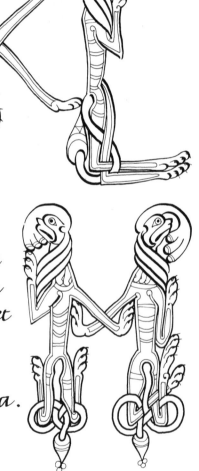

In this alphabet, we
have no J, K, or M, in
fact a whole alphabet
may be derived from
a single letter, as
these five from fig. 82 a.

Fig. 82   Monogram IN, a ; Irish uncial N, b.

 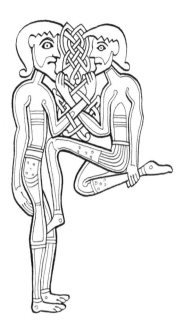

a   b

Three lions
with scrolled manes
and
ribbed flanks.   Two men.

FIG.83

*Two lions with split ribbon necks and waists tied
in Josephine knots.*

Fig. 84   Monogram PA, with uncial A.

Two lions.

FIG. 85

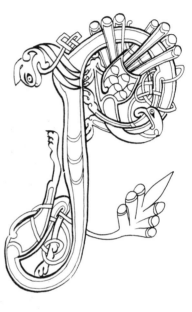

a   b

Two lions.
The descender could   Lion and bird.
double as a J.   Lion's tail has ringlets.

Fíg.86

a   b

Two lions.   Two lions and an eagle.

Fï5. 87

This letter has a serrated edge, and also an
unusual curl for a serif.

Fig. 88

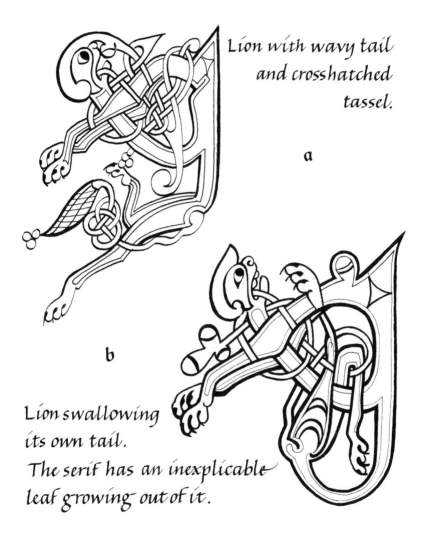

Lion with wavy tail
and crosshatched
tassel.

a

b

Lion swallowing
its own tail.
The serif has an inexplicable
leaf growing out of it.

Fig.89

Opposite:

a Human figure with single leg.
b Human figure with beard-and-tongue knot.

Below:

Two lionesses and bird. The hooped cat has the cheek bars that signify whiskers.

FIG.90

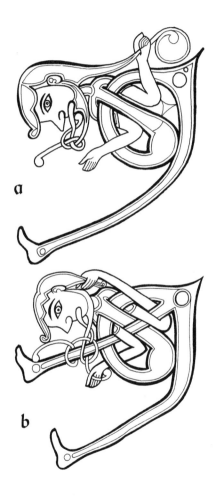

a

b

FIG. 91

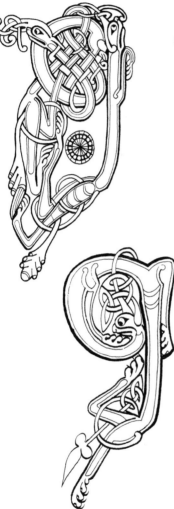

a

Two lions.
Separated,
they make a C and J.

Lion.

b

Fís. 92

Lion with full-maned lion head serif.

Fig.93   Monogram SI.

Two lions.
The lion of the I has a trilobe mane.

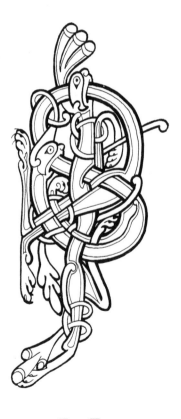

Fig.94

Lion suffocating a bird.

Fig. 95

Lion with trefoil
tail,

a

Lion with trefoil tail adapted to a
monogram.

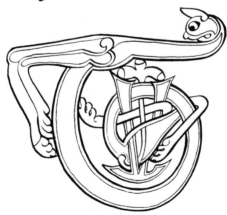

b

Lion suffocating a bird.

a

Lion with triangular extension on the curve.

b

Fig. 97

Two lionesses.

FIȝ.98

Two serpents with manes.

Fig.99

Opposed lions with tongues tied in a knot.

❋

ANIMAL AMPERSANDS

 MATCHING SET of amper‑
sands, belonging with the
previous alphabet, filled
with snakes and birds, displays the ver‑
satility of this form of lettering, here
verging on the boundary between charac‑
ter and decoration. In fact, these designs
are sometimes mistaken for ornaments
in themselves, taken out of context and
used as part of a border, or as jewelry
motifs. Enlarged, they make good de‑
cals also.

Fig. 100

One snake.

M OST OF THESE ANIMAL AMP-
ersands take the form of the
so-called snake of Celtic art. It was a
latecomer to the repertory of ornament,
a speciality of the Book of Kells, or one
of the artists of that Book. Even in the
kells animal alphabet, the snake is not
much used, compared to the lion and
the eagle. Exceptions are *figs 75a, 76b, 98.*

fig.101

Two snakes biting.

I N THE ALPHABET of DECORATED letters,
chapter III, there are no snakes either,
but in chapter IV it occurs in *fig. 62b*.
There it appears in a very simple form.
The form is quite definite, though: the
head is shown from above, the eyes set in
two touching lobes which may be drawn
out into freehand knots; a third lobe
provides the creature with a bill or snout

[*137*]

Fig. 102

Two snakes and a fish.

that may be treated in a variety of ways; and the creature's body ends in a tail, also amenable to variation. In fig. 102, the tails are fishy crescents, one tipped with little balls, the other joined to its owner's snout, as if being chewed. Except the tail is not that of the nibbler. It belongs to the head with its tongue licking out across its flexed gill lappet.

fig. 103

Two snakes .

IN *fig.* 103, each snake may be read as one of the letters ᴇᴄ. The former has its right ear bent sharply under its throat. It bites on the other ear, also sharply bent, but forward; the latter has ear lappets crossing its neck. Both have an ear terminating in a foliate tassel, similar to the lion's tail of *fig.*104. Here the bird's crest curves forward and

Fig.104

palmates in three lobes such as used for
the ringlets of the lions' forelocks, as
in fig.82. The treatment of lion mane

Lion biting bird?

and bird crest is carried over to the
treatment of the snake's head and tail
fin lappet, suggesting further such
adaptations to an as yet unrealised snake
alphabet. Compare the ears of figs 101

Fig .105

and 75 ; or snout and tail fin of *fig*.105
with that of *fig.* 76 b.

Two snakes.

Fig. 76 b has a teardrop on its nose, like
*fig.*105 . Both have triplex tails, the
former a crescent-and-spike; the latter,
however is a further development, intro-

ducing the cat's-paw motif of fig.15 as
an alternative tail fin for the snake. In
fig. 105 the snake's topknot is fully devel-

Single snake with fishtail.

oped fore-and-aft, like the mane of fig.75b.
In figs 103-107 the snakes have borrowed a
shoulder bulge from a lion as at fig.104.
Finally , the mane treatment of fig.78b,
with its toenailed lobes, as well as the

fig. 107

trefoil tail tassels of *fig. 75b* come to-
gether in the gill-lappets of *fig.107*, one
of which has a secondary ringlet lobe.

Two-headed snake.

These leonine ringlets and tassels, so like
foliage, are the basis of the Irish Urnes
style of the dawning Viking age. They
were the Animal Style master's swan
song: the fourth and final part of the
Book of Kells lacks his astounding legacy.

[143]

FIG. 108   Set of riveted ampersands.

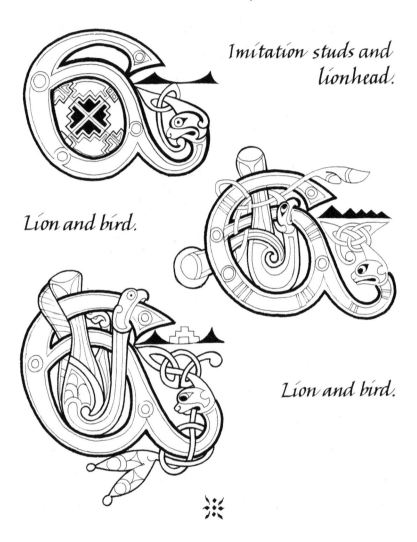

Imitation studs and
lionhead.

Lion and bird.

Lion and bird.

ANGULAR CAPITALS

NE OF THE LEAST KNOWN yet most excitingly malleable Celtic scripts, these decorative capitals were created as a display alphabet by the illuminators of the mid-seventh century Columban or Irish scriptoria. They no doubt felt the need to have a third type of script to make up for the birth of minuscule script – equivalent to our modern lower-er case lettering– as an alternative to majuscule, half uncial, which hither-to served as text as well as display script.

[145]

Fig. 109 Angular alphabet.

Fig. 110 Beginning of Luke, Lichfield.

Lichfield Gospel Book, folio 221, Luke 1:1.
quidem multi conati sunt ordinare...

[147]

Fig.111   Beginning of Matthew, Lindisfarne.

Lindisfarne, folio 27. Math. 1:1. (Liber) generationis IHU XPI, filii David, filii Abraham.

Fig. 112   Beginning of Mark, Lindisfarne.

Lindisfarne, folio 95.
Mark 1 : 1, 2.
Initium evangelii
I·H·U X·P·I filii dei.
Sicut scribtum est..

(ini)t   i   u+m.

e   v   a+n-

g   e   l   i·I·H·U.

x   p   i·f·i·l·i·D·i·s·i·cut·

s   c   r   i   b   t   u   m·e·s·t†

Fig.113   Beginning of Luke, Lindisfarne.

Lindisfarne, fol.139.
folio 139. Luke 1:1.
(Q) uoniam quidem
multi conati sunt
ordinare narrationem
Forasmuch as many
have taken in hand to
set forth a declaration.

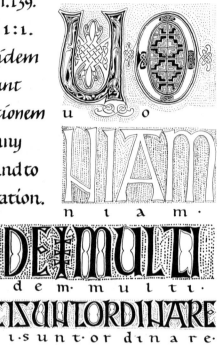

FIG.114   Beginning of John, Lindisfarne.

The Book of Lindisfarne, folio 211;
beginning of the Gospel of St John:
(In p) rincipio erat verbum et verbum erat apud
dominum et deus (erat verbum)

The smaller letters are 8-10 nibwidths high.

Fig. 115   Angular knotwork letters, Kells.

KELLS
FOLIO 183 R

(E) rat autem hora tercia

Mark 15 : 25

(e)   r   a   t .

a   u   t+e m.

h+o   r   a · t e r cia·

FIG.116 Angular outlined letters, Kells.

**KELLS
FOLIO 124 R**

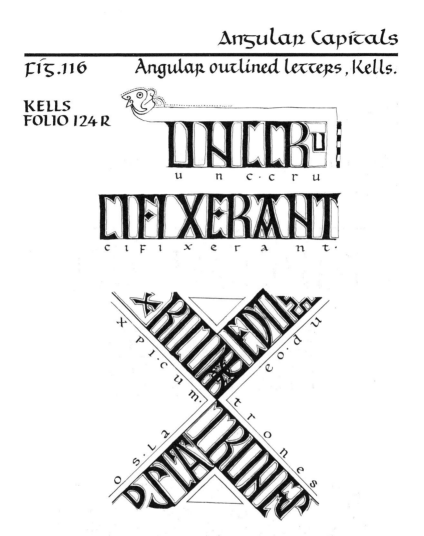

u   n c·cru

cifixerant·

x pi·cum· latrones eodu osla

(T) unc cru-cifixerunt XPI cum eo duos latrones
Matt. 27:38

Fig. 117

**KELLS
FOLIO 292 R**

(In princi) pio erat verbum verum.

John 1:1

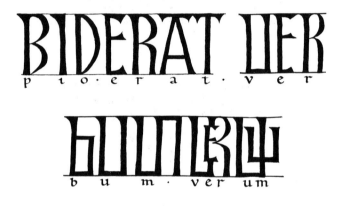

Fig.118 Interspace filling

KELLS FOLIO 285R

Autem sabbati valde de lu(culo). **Luke 26:1**

a u t e m · s a b

b a t i · u a l d e d e l u-

KELLS FOLIO 29R stacked title block.

[Liber]
generationis

Fig.119

KELLS FOLIO 8R

XPIInBETRLEM Iu
x p i i n b e t h l e m . Ju-

ꝺEꜺEMꜺꞀ
d e a e . M a g i

ꜰꞀuNERAOꝔꝔERUNT B
m u n e r a · o f f e r u n t · &

IIꞀꝼꜺNTEꞂINꞂR
i i n f a n t e s i n ter ~

ꝼICIUNTUR ꞂETRESSID
f i c i u n t u r · r e g r e s s i o ·

THE QUICK BROWN FOX JUMPS OVER THE LAZY DOG
THE·QUICK·BROWN·FOX·JUMPS·OVER·THE·LAZY·DOG

DETAIL of decorative border, folio 285 R

Glossary of terms

DECAL. A design transferred onto the back of a jacket.

FYLFOT. The Saxon term for swastika.

KEY PATTERN. Celtic fret pattern: diagonal, interlocking angular paths resembling L-shaped slots cut in keys. See Beginners' Manual, Ch.II.

LAPPET. Literally, a loose, hanging part of something; a secondary ribbon or knot extending from a main figure in an animal pattern, as an ear, tongue or tail.

LENTOID. Shaped like a lens, or lentil.

MEROVINGIAN. The first Frankish dynasty, c. 500 - 750.

PELTA.   Term for a classic motif that
is derived from the form of a palm leaf,
shaped like a fan, the outer corners of
which may be elaborated into spirals.

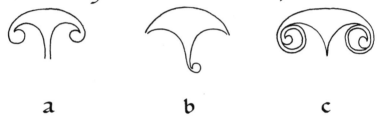

a   b   c

SALTIRE. Diagonal cross.
STEP PATTERN. Straight lines bent like
the steps of a stair; see Beginner's Manual.
TRIQUETRA.   Simple triangular knot
with a continuous path, very simple and
fun to do, which is what makes it the
most popular Celtic knot to this day. It
may be constructed by the scribe's method
in two ways, open or closed form.

See Appendix to Knotwork for 60 triquetras.
Open form:

Closed form:

Split-ribbon form:

TRISKELE. *A spiral whirligig with three arms; also spelt 'triskel'.*

Triskele:

Appendix

Recommended List of Books to Read

Janet Backhouse,
The Lindisfarne Gospels, Oxford 1981

Françoise Henry,
Irish Art, London 1970
___ *The Book of Kells*, London 1974

Aidan Meehan,
Celtic Design: A Beginner's Manual,
London 1991
___ *Celtic Design: Knotwork*, London 1991
___ *Celtic Design: Animal Patterns*,
London 1992

Carl Nordenfalk,
Celtic and Anglo-Saxon Painting
London 1977

✳